D0593408

PAUSE

100 Moments of Calm

summersdale

PAUSE

Copyright © Summersdale Publishers Ltd, 2019

Text by Poppy O'Neill

All rights reserved.

No part of this book may be reproduced by any means, nor transmitted, nor translated into a machine language, without the written permission of the publishers.

Condition of Sale
This book is sold subject to the condition that it shall not, by way of trade or otherwise, be lent, resold, hired out or otherwise circulated in any form of binding or cover other than that in which it is published and without a similar condition including this condition being imposed on the subsequent purchaser.

An Hachette UK Company
www.hachette.co.uk

Summersdale Publishers Ltd
Part of Octopus Publishing Group Limited
Carmelite House
50 Victoria Embankment
LONDON
EC4Y 0DZ
UK

www.summersdale.com

Printed and bound in China

ISBN: 978-1-78685-948-8

Substantial discounts on bulk quantities of Summersdale books are available to corporations, professional associations and other organizations. For details contact general enquiries: telephone: +44 (0) 1243 771107 or email: enquiries@summersdale.com.

TO..................

FROM..............

1

Breathe: deep breathing can help release tension in your body, reduce heart rate and regulate your brain's levels of serotonin – the neurotransmitter linked to feelings of happiness and well-being.

Breathe in through your nose for a count of five, hold for five, then breathe out through your mouth, making a sighing noise. Use your abdominal muscles to gently and completely empty your lungs.

2

Make a self-care playlist of soothing music to enjoy on your way to work and begin the day feeling relaxed and calm. Classical pieces or chill-out acoustic tunes will help set a serene tone for your journey and even provide a background to allow you to approach your commute mindfully.

3. GET SOME INDOOR GREENERY

House plants require patience, which is the essence of a calm lifestyle. Having plants around the house also improves air quality and they're a beautiful addition to any room. Take care picking the perfect location and pot for your new plant and enjoy its slow unfolding.

Best houseplants for a calmer atmosphere:

- **Aloe vera** – purifies the air and can be used as a natural remedy to soothe burns and other skin conditions.

- **Rubber plant** – super-low maintenance and ideally suited to cooler climates. Watch how the leaves gradually unfurl from a central red spine into a shiny dark-green oval.

- **Snake plant** – scientists at NASA found that having one of these easy-to-care-for plants in your home lowers toxins in the air as well as reducing anxiety.

- **Bamboo palm** – another air-cleaning superhero, fast-growing bamboo makes a graceful addition to your living room or office.

4

Write a thank you letter. Expressing gratitude is incredibly therapeutic – evidence suggests that grateful people experience higher levels of positive emotions such as joy, happiness and optimism. Writing an old-fashioned letter means you'll take the time to think about what you're going to say first, before writing it out.

WHATEVER
IS YOURS WILL
ALWAYS BE YOURS,
WHATEVER MOVES
AWAY WAS NEVER
YOURS BEFORE.

SRI SRI RAVI SHANKAR

5

Practise mindful eating. Listen to your body and eat only when you are hungry. Eat slowly, savouring every mouthful and stopping when you feel satisfied – not only will you feel calmer, but you will digest your food more easily. Consider the life cycle of the food you're eating, and all the energy and work that has gone into your meal.

6

Embrace stillness. Not everything in your life requires a response or reaction from you. Sometimes the best course of action is no action: take a step back and let it be. There is power in observing how things unfold rather than attempting to control external events.

7

Go for a walk on your own. Take time to be alone with your thoughts, breathe in the fresh air and appreciate the beauty of your surroundings. Whether you're climbing a mountain or simply taking the scenic route home from work, learning to slow down and enjoy your own company is one of the most valuable gifts you can give yourself.

8. DECLUTTER YOUR ONLINE SPACE

We spend so much of our waking lives online these days, so make sure your online life is as calm as possible, and that you're not wasting time and energy on things that stress you out or don't interest you.

Tips for a peaceful online life:

- Turn off push notifications.

- Uninstall non-essential apps.

- Delete old files.

- Log out of social media at the end of every session.

- Clear your cookies.

- Unsubscribe from spam newsletters.

- Take time to be offline every day.

- Give yourself down time when you are eating.

- Aim for no screen time for an hour before bed.

- Never let your device enter the sanctuary of your bedroom.

YOUR MIND WILL ANSWER MOST QUESTIONS IF YOU LEARN TO RELAX AND WAIT FOR THE ANSWER.

WILLIAM S. BURROUGHS

9

Track your mood. Download a mood-tracker app or make a note in your diary each day about how you are feeling. We don't often give ourselves the opportunity to monitor these things so this is a great way to put your emotions in perspective and to notice patterns and any stress points.

10

Stare out of the window. Whether you have a view of a busy street or rolling fields, zoning out and letting your mind wander is a great way to add a brief pause to whatever you're doing. We're often at our most creative when we're calm and thoughts can come and go freely.

11

Self-care is just as important as life's other necessities, so schedule in a walk or a long soak in the tub as often as you can and stick to it just as you would any other appointment. Prioritizing yourself in this way might feel self-indulgent at first, so try to ignore your inner critic. When you tend to your own needs with love and patience, you become the best possible version of yourself.

12

Smile :) The physical act of smiling activates neural pathways linked to happiness and well-being. Like a natural anti-depressant, mood-boosting neurotransmitters dopamine and serotonin are released when you smile. Try smiling to yourself right now, or next time you look in the mirror, and notice the difference it makes to your mood. Say cheese!

Look at the
night sky and
talk to the
universe.

13. REDUCE YOUR CAFFEINE INTAKE

Caffeine is known to be a stimulant so give yourself a break and try swapping out your usual coffee or tea for these alternatives:

- **Rooibos** – this South African staple is naturally caffeine-free but has a similar earthiness to English Breakfast. It's also packed with antioxidants, vitamins and minerals.

- **Camomile** – a classic bedtime drink, this delicate tea is made from daisy-like camomile flower heads and will help you drift off more easily.

- **Green tea** – while there is caffeine in green tea, it contains a lot less than black tea so is a good choice if you're looking to reduce your caffeine intake rather than cut it out completely.

- **Peppermint** – this tea is great for your digestion and calming for your body and mind, thanks to the menthol in peppermint leaves acting as a natural muscle relaxant.

Nothing
is wrong –
whatever is
happening is
just "real life".

TARA BRACH

14

Visit an art gallery. Move round slowly, taking in each work of art and noticing how it makes you feel. Embrace the peace and quiet that descends in a gallery and make the most of the gentle pace that others seem to observe as they wander between exhibits, taking the time to consider each work.

15

Make your favourite meal from scratch. Source good quality, fresh ingredients and really take your time over the preparation. Stews and curries are great for slow, mindful cooking with zero stress, and the sense of accomplishment when you serve up and take that first bite is so worth it.

16

Have a good cry. Keeping your emotions bottled up is never a good idea. Crying is not a sign of weakness; it is simply a physical way to release emotions. Tears are how your body releases stress hormones – they are quite literally a valve for letting go of negative emotions such as sadness, grief and anxiety. Find a safe place and let yourself really feel your feelings.

17

Learn to say no. Setting boundaries is an incredibly useful skill that will improve your life immeasurably and allow you to take more control. It's how you protect your inner peace by choosing what you do and when. If you don't want to go out – don't. Opt for a quiet night in. Remember, if someone is upset by you asserting your boundaries, it is not your responsibility to appease them: "no" is a complete sentence.

Rise above other people's nonsense.

18. MOVE YOUR BODY

Improved health, channelling nervous energy and releasing feel-good endorphins – the benefits of physical exercise are well known.

Recent studies show regular exercise creates new brain cells that boost the speed at which we are able to calm down after experiencing something stressful.

Whether it's the community and accountability of a team sport, the peace of solitary running or the gentle routine of a weekly yoga class, find a form of exercise that fits with your lifestyle and personality, and commit to it. There are plenty of apps to help you get started if you're struggling to find a fitness direction. Take the challenge and find what suits you – you really will not regret it.

GRANT ME THE SERENITY
TO ACCEPT THE THINGS
I CANNOT CHANGE;
COURAGE TO CHANGE
THE THINGS I CAN; AND
WISDOM TO KNOW
THE DIFFERENCE.

REINHOLD NIEBUHR

19

Do one thing at a time, slowly and deliberately. When you're busy or multi-tasking it might feel like you're being effective, but you're actually just needlessly stressing yourself out, and you run the risk of forgetting or neglecting some of your responsibilities. The most efficient way of getting things done is to act mindfully and methodically, giving each task your full attention.

20

Even the most stressful experiences bring unexpected gifts. It can be hard to see the positive sometimes, so considering what you've learned from what you've been through can help you grow as a person and look back with gratitude and peace.

21

Embrace JOMO – aka the joy of
missing out. JOMO comes when
you cancel plans in order to stay in,
veg out and generally do as little as
humanly possible. How luxurious to
wallow in the comfort of your bed
with a good book for company! If
you don't see time spent relaxing
at home as wasted, it becomes
desirable and valuable self-care.

22

Reading the right poem at the right moment can be incredibly therapeutic. Seek out anthologies of poetry for calm and tranquillity, or search online. In poetry, every word has to count so you can really take your time over reading. One poem at a time is enough, and a good one will stay with you all day. If you're feeling inspired, you could try writing your own.

YOU ARE YOUR
BEST THING.

TONI MORRISON

23. DECLUTTER
   YOUR WARDROBE

You know the feeling: you open your wardrobe and see a mess staring back – the perfect black top you wanted to wear is buried somewhere within and probably creased up like an old tissue.

It's time for a sort-out.

Put out-of-season clothes away neatly, keeping your clothes in better condition and making getting dressed in the morning that much easier.

Get rid of anything that doesn't fit or you haven't worn in the last 18 months by donating it to charity or taking it to a textile recycling bank. Even better, organize a clothes swap evening with your friends and come away with new, free clothes!

24

A tidy environment helps create a calm mind. Start with the space around you right now – find something to put away, something to throw away and something to clean. Tackle one room, cupboard or corner at a time and enjoy the satisfaction a little methodical tidying will bring.

25

Turn off your phone for half an hour. Whether you feel like you get too many notifications or too few, phones are stressful, demanding little beasts and it's a good idea to take a regular break from their presence. The world will not end if you are un-contactable for a short time each day – enjoy the silence!

26

Everybody loves a good stretch – try reaching up as high as you can, then roll downwards and touch your toes. To your muscles, a stretch is as good as a massage because it actively releases tension, leading to a more relaxed body and mind. Stretching has also been found to improve sleep quality and circulation and make exercise more effective.

SIMPLY LET EXPERIENCE
TAKE PLACE VERY FREELY,
SO THAT YOUR OPEN HEART
IS SUFFUSED WITH THE
TENDERNESS OF TRUE
COMPASSION.

TSOKNYI RINPOCHE

27

Visit the sea – whatever the weather. Let yourself be mesmerized by the rhythmic churn of the waves, the slow coming and going of the tide and the quality of the air. What's more, the negative ions in sea air accelerate your ability to absorb oxygen and balance your serotonin levels, leading to reduced stress and improved mood. Try throwing stones into the water, imagining that each one represents something you want to let go of.

28

Change your sheets – nothing
feels better than getting into a
freshly made bed after a long day.
The smell... the smoothness... it's
one of life's great simple pleasures,
and so worth the effort. Why
not sprinkle some lavender oil on
your pillow as a finishing touch?

29. ALLOW YOURSELF TO FEEL ANGRY

Anger is an emotion like any other, but one we can feel ashamed of or uncomfortable with. Feeling angry is often a sign we've been treated in a way we didn't deserve and shows healthy self-esteem. If you squash it down or resist it, anger will always come out eventually.

Perhaps counter-intuitively, the best way to deal with anger (as with any emotion) is to allow yourself to feel it. While it's rarely a good idea to act out of anger, if you simply allow the feeling to exist and listen to yourself when it arises, the emotion will pass more quickly.

Try writing your angry thoughts on paper and either ripping them up, burning them or submerging them in water, washing the words away.

30

Designate a period of quiet time for everyone in your house each day. Take half an hour to switch off all screens and engage in quiet hobbies such as reading, meditation, gardening or doing a jigsaw puzzle. Taking a break from technology and work helps reduce stress and has actually been shown to boost productivity.

SMILE, BREATHE
AND GO SLOWLY.

THÍCH NHẤT HẠNH

31

You don't have to be an artist with a capital "A" to make something beautiful and worthwhile. Creativity is something that everyone is capable of and expressing ourselves creatively has a huge impact on our emotional and mental well-being.

Try creating...

A photograph

A flower mandala

A delicious meal

A tidy room

A heartfelt letter

A lush garden

A thoughtful birthday present

32

Go to the cinema and take a break from reality by immersing yourself in a film. When you give your full attention to a piece of cinema, you can put any real-world stresses on hold, enjoy the emotional experience of the film and just relax for a couple of hours.

I am a better person when I have less on my plate.

ELIZABETH GILBERT

33

Rescue fond memories from digital limbo by having your favourite photos printed. Take your time picking out the perfect frame and a great spot for them in your home. Once they're up, you'll enjoy a reminder of that happy moment every time you pass by.

34. TRY AFFIRMATIONS

Exposing yourself regularly to positive affirmations imprints these messages onto your subconscious mind. To create the most powerful affirmations, use positive language (i.e. say what you want, not what you don't want), in the present tense, even if it's something you're working towards or find hard to believe about yourself right now.

Write your affirmations down and say them in front of the mirror as often as you can. Here are a few ideas to get you started:

- I am worthy.

- I am lucky.

- I am calm.

- I am strong.

- I am healthy.

- I am in control of my life.

- I am enough.

THE SECRET OF SUCCESS
IS TO BE IN HARMONY
WITH EXISTENCE, TO BE
ALWAYS CALM AND TO LET
EACH WAVE OF LIFE WASH
US A LITTLE FARTHER
UP THE SHORE.

CYRIL CONNOLLY

35

Unfollow, unfriend, block. Social media is meant to be fun and informative! If the sight of a particular account or person's posts on your feed stresses you out, feel no guilt in removing them in the way that feels most comfortable to you. Life's too short to give attention to anything that depletes your inner peace.

Imagine roots growing
from the soles of your feet
into the ground, anchoring
and supporting you.

36

Try setting your alarm five minutes earlier. You'll be amazed at the difference it makes – five extra minutes could let you linger over breakfast, stay longer in the shower or meditate before you leave the house. A less stressful morning will set you up for a positive, calm day.

37

Listen to a guided meditation while doing mundane chores. Busy hands can help focus your mind, and a bit of distraction makes those boring jobs go quicker. Just because you're not sitting still with your eyes closed doesn't mean you won't feel some of the benefits of a guided meditation. Try an app like Insight Timer or Headspace, and allow the calm, positive messages to reach your mind and give you a new perspective on life.

Accept people for who they are, including *yourself.*

38. PRACTISE GRATITUDE

Make a list of three things you're grateful for – big or small. Expressing gratitude focuses your mind on the positive things in your life. You could keep your gratitude list in a journal or diary, or write each entry on a scrap of paper and keep them in a jar.

Studies show that a regular gratitude practice increases resilience, strengthens relationships, improves sleep quality and reduces stress.

Add three new things every day, directing your attention towards all the beauty in your life, and soon enough you'll train your mind to find the good even in stressful or negative experiences.

Here are a few to inspire you:

- I'm grateful for plans with good friends.

- I'm grateful for sunlight.

- I'm grateful this cold is prompting me to rest my body.

YOU DON'T NEED STRENGTH TO LET GO OF SOMETHING. WHAT YOU REALLY NEED IS UNDERSTANDING.

GUY FINLEY

39

Read a book. Most of us are in the habit of scrolling through our phones during idle moments. Instead, pick up a book – you can ignore what's going on around you and get lost in a different world. Get to know the characters and enjoy the gradual unfolding of a story.

40

Go outside: a dose of fresh air and sunlight every day works wonders for your mental health, mood, sleep habits and sense of well-being. When outdoors, you're naturally more able to be in the moment while you appreciate and wonder at your surroundings. Plus, research shows that vitamin D – absorbed into the body from sunlight – might play an important role in regulating mood and warding off depression.

41

Don't make wishes – set intentions. In order to feel calmly in control of your life, set achievable goals and take steps towards them. Be mindful about what you say "yes" and "no" to, asking yourself if this choice will take you in the direction you want to go in. Once you've worked out your intentions, make them more real by writing them down or creating a vision board. Take time every day to revisit your intentions and picture how you will feel when you achieve your dreams.

42

Let your playful side shine. Remember how you were as a carefree child living in the moment, excited and enthusiastic to experience things just for fun.

Here are some playful ideas to try:

- Dance in the kitchen
- Sing to your pets
- Lie on your back outside and cloud spot – what shapes do you see?
- Jump over waves

43

Jot down your dreams; they are a window into your subconscious and can tell you a lot about what's really going on in your mind. Use a dream dictionary or simply rely on your own intuition to interpret their meanings. Try to write down everything you can remember – including the emotions you felt – before it disappears from your mind.

44. PLAY WITH COLOUR

Get your paints out and experiment with colour and shape on the page. Colouring in has been found to have the same health benefits as meditation, allowing your brain to switch off and focus on one thing, which in turn reduces anxiety and restores a sense of well-being.

Regularly indulging in a simple, creative activity such as painting or colouring is a powerful tool towards creating a calmer you.

WITHIN YOU, THERE
IS A STILLNESS AND A
SANCTUARY TO WHICH
YOU CAN RETREAT AT ANY
TIME AND BE YOURSELF.

HERMANN HESSE

45

Take care of your gut. Scientists are finding an ever-closer link between a healthy gut and a healthy mind. Eating lots of fibre-rich foods and taking a probiotic help ensure healthy gut bacteria and better overall physical and mental health. A plentiful, diverse mix of gut bacteria helps optimize the body's response to stress by producing serotonin and other mood-regulating neurotransmitters. When your gut is working well, these neurotransmitters help bring calm and clarity to your mind in times of mental turmoil.

46

Do small favours for others and expect nothing in return. Random acts of kindness don't give just the recipient the warm and fuzzies! Benefits of demonstrating no-strings kindness towards others range from increased feel-good brain chemicals serotonin and oxytocin to improved energy and even a longer lifespan. Being kind on a regular basis has also been found to reduce levels of stress, anxiety and depression.

47

Treat your skin to a home-made face mask. For soft, nourished skin, simply combine these ingredients to form a paste:

¼ ripe avocado, mashed
1 tbsp coconut oil
1 tsp oats
3 drops tea tree oil

Apply the mask to clean, dry skin and relax for ten minutes. Wipe away the oats with cotton wool (so as not to block your sink – it can get quite messy!) then rinse your face with warm water and pat dry with a towel.

48

Go to bed early – a well-rested mind is better prepared for whatever the day has in store. The more sleep you get, the more you will be able to stay in control of your emotions and keep things in perspective. Find out what works for you – most people need between seven and nine hours to feel energized and ready for anything life might throw their way.

Have
patience.

49. TAPPING THERAPY

Combining the Chinese art of acupressure with modern psychology, "tapping" focuses on specific parts of your body combined with positive self-talk. A regular tapping practice can be an effective way to reduce stress.

Tapping works in a similar way to acupuncture, by stimulating the points believed to be connected to the body's energy centres. The ritual nature of rhythmic tapping alongside positive affirmations works to re-programme your mind and help control your emotions.

Start by gently tapping the outer side of your hand with the tips of your index and middle fingers, saying: "Even though [your problem], I accept myself." For example: "Even though I feel stressed about work, I accept myself."

Then tap the top of your head, your eyebrow, the area next to and under your eye, under your nose, your chin, your collarbone and under your arm, repeating the same affirmation with each tap. Finish with a deep breath.

Nothing can bring you peace but yourself.

RALPH WALDO EMERSON

50

Making decisions can cause stress levels to rise, and it's easy to over-think things and end up tying yourself in knots. Next time you have to make a difficult choice, follow these steps:

- Breathe, relax.
- Remind yourself that whatever happens, things will work out. Even mistakes can hold valuable lessons.
- Check in with yourself – what is your gut instinct? Go with that.

51

Go on a date with yourself. Take yourself to your favourite coffee shop, go rock-climbing, go on a country walk, or to a restaurant you love... the most important relationship in your life is the one you have with yourself. Feeling secure and happy in your own company is key to a calm, resilient mind, so celebrate and cultivate your alone time.

52

Get organized for tomorrow before you go to bed. If you have a hectic morning routine, think about which parts you could do in advance. Spending a little time getting sorted in the evening will free up precious minutes in the morning, making your whole routine that bit more relaxed.

53

Do the thing you've been putting off. You know the thing. It's small, but there's something about it that fills you with anxiety, so it keeps going to the bottom of your to-do list. So... just do it! Make that appointment, clear out that drawer, write that email. You'll feel so much better without it weighing on your mind.

Remain calm in every situation because peace equals power.

JOYCE MEYER

54. FREE HUGS!

Author and therapist Virginia Satir says we need four hugs a day for survival, eight hugs for maintenance and 12 for growth.

Physical contact is a basic human need, essential for our emotional and mental well-being. A hug from the right person at the right time can help reduce stress and anxiety, as well as lifting mood and fostering connection. Research shows that a hug needs to be at least 20 seconds long to get the maximum benefits.

The best thing about a hug is that it's almost impossible to give one without receiving one. If you're not a natural hugger, try offering a hug to someone you are close to and comfortable with once a day and go from there.

"

PERFECT TRANQUILLITY
WITHIN CONSISTS IN
THE GOOD ORDERING
OF THE MIND, THE
REALM OF YOUR OWN.

MARCUS AURELIUS

55

Be nice to strangers, exuding calm
and warmth as you go about your
day. You never know what sort of
day anyone else is having, so never
take others' behaviour personally.
A bit of kindness can lift someone's
spirits in ways you'll never know,
so leave everybody you encounter
a little better than you found
them, safe in the knowledge that
karma will have your back if you're
ever in need of a little kindness.

56

Shinrin-yoku – aka forest bathing – is the Japanese theory and practice of taking in the healing atmosphere of the forest. It's been found to improve immunity and lower levels of the stress hormone cortisol.

Next time you're in the woods, walk slowly and observe the earthy scent, the silence under a leafy canopy and the serenity of green leaves. Feel the texture of bark and moss. Breathe deeply and open all your senses to your surroundings.

57

It's almost impossible to drink
too much water, and the more
you drink, the better you'll feel.
Low water intake is linked to low
mood, headaches and fatigue
so make sure you get at least a
couple of litres a day. Get into the
habit of carrying a water bottle
with you and fill up regularly.

58

Trust the process and let go with grace. If someone or something is leaving your life, try not to cling or resist. Don't be afraid to communicate your needs – be clear and honest and you'll have no regrets. Then if it goes, let it go and grieve at your own pace. New things will come and time will heal.

Stop and smell the flowers.

59. KEEP A "NO-FILTER" JOURNAL

Journaling helps relieve stress and anxiety by allowing you to express your thoughts and feelings in a safe, judgement-free way. Writing your thoughts down creates order when your mind feels chaotic – it's easier to see which thoughts aren't helping you when you get them down on paper. No one will read your journal – perhaps not even you! So you can be free to write exactly what you're thinking and how you feel.

Try these questions to start you off:

- How do I feel right now?

- What is going well in my life?

- What's taking up most of my mental energy?

- What can I do to take better care of myself?

EACH PERSON
DESERVES A DAY IN
WHICH NO PROBLEMS
ARE CONFRONTED,
NO SOLUTIONS
SEARCHED FOR.

MAYA ANGELOU

60

Ground yourself. Walking barefoot on grass, soil or sand grounds you, putting you in touch with the earth's natural energy and bringing your attention out of your mind and into your body. As you feel the ground beneath your feet, pay attention to the textures and sensations, taking slow, deliberate steps.

61

Make a space in your home just for you. Keep it tidy and sacred, and decorate your space with beautiful objects like crystals, candles and plants. Have room in your space for your favourite feel-good films, novels, comfiest blankets, scented candles – whatever makes you feel good. Make it your go-to spot for whenever you need to recharge.

Stop a moment, cease your work, look around you.

LEO TOLSTOY

62

Watch a fire – whether a single candle flame or a crackling bonfire, get mesmerized by its beautiful, ever-changing nature. Some scientists believe that the relaxing, hypnotic effect of an open flame may be down to the evolutionary benefits of fire – providing social bonding, warmth and light, and warding off predators and insects.

63

Life's too short to worry about blending in or saving things for "best": wear only the clothes you feel comfortable and fabulous in. Dressing well doesn't have to mean dressing smartly; it means dressing so that you look and feel like yourself. Some days that might mean a mood-lifting brightly coloured top, other days it'll be a fleecy onesie. Putting on an outfit you feel good in will set you up for the day and help you feel calm and in control.

64. GET INTO THE HABIT OF MEDITATING

Making time regularly to be still, silent and alone with your thoughts will help you become more self-aware and emotionally resilient, as well as reducing stress and anxiety.

Find a spot where you can sit comfortably and won't be disturbed. Set a timer for how long you'd like to meditate – it could be as little as five minutes.

Take three deep breaths and close your eyes. Breathing normally, bring your awareness to the top of your head, noticing any sensations you feel there.

Let your attention travel slowly down your body, checking in with every feeling or sensation you come across. Keep going all the way to your toes.

If you get distracted, don't worry! Just bring your attention gently back to your breath and carry on.

Once the time's up, take one more deep breath before slowly returning to your day.

What other
people think
of me is
none of my
business.

WAYNE DYER

65

If you're facing a difficult new challenge, don't stress! Cultivate a beginner's mindset, where you approach everything with a calm curiosity and willingness to be taught. There will always be something new to learn, even in the things you're most familiar with – enjoy that prospect and let go of the need to be perfect all the time.

66

Grow something: houseplants, vegetables, herbs, flowers... the sight of life unfolding slowly before your eyes is a beautiful reminder of the need for patience and the power of calm, unhurried progress. Grow from a seed or get some cuttings from a friend and try water propagation.

67

Just being around certain animals can have an instant calming effect. In fact, stroking a pet has been proven to lower heart rate and blood pressure, reducing stress and increasing a sense of well-being.

If you don't have animals at home, try borrowing a friend's dog for the afternoon or search your local area for organizations offering activities such as alpaca walking or birdwatching, or spend some time in a cat cafe.

68

It's time to prioritize. What needs doing now? What can wait until later? What can you let go of? Once you learn the skill of prioritization, you'll find your to-do list a lot more manageable, enabling you to focus on one task at a time. Before you know it, you'll feel calmer and more in control of your life.

Go with the
flow.

69. SET BOUNDARIES WITH OTHERS

Work out where your boundaries are and give less of your attention to people who are toxic to you. If someone in your life treats you badly or their actions make you feel insecure, anxious or miserable, take steps to distance yourself from them. Be mindful of how you feel when you are with someone or just after – if you feel negative emotions then question why that is: is it you, the situation or them?

You don't have to cut people out of your life completely – boundaries are intensely personal. *You* decide where your boundaries lie and how much of your attention and energy to give to different people.

THERE ARE DAYS I DROP
WORDS OF COMFORT
LIKE FALLING LEAVES
AND REMEMBER THAT IT
IS ENOUGH TO BE TAKEN
CARE OF BY MYSELF.

BRIAN ANDREAS

70

Go for a walk in good company.
Get out of the house and enjoy
some scenic beauty with a family
member or close friend. Walking
reduces stress levels and enhances
psychological well-being. And,
not only will the gentle exercise
do you good, it'll strengthen your
relationship too. Plus, it's free!

71

Donating your time, money or resources to charity benefits those in need, but it also benefits the giver. Altruistic giving activates your brain's pleasure response, releasing a surge of feel-good endorphins and dopamine. It's OK to feel good about giving to charity, and doing your bit will make a difference. Try a sponsored run, volunteering your time or donating unwanted clothes to your local charity shop.

72

Write negative thoughts on toilet paper. It helps to get negative or stressful thoughts out of your head and onto paper, and using *this* kind of paper takes away any seriousness attached to them. Negative thoughts don't do you any good, so why not just flush them away?

73

Look at your average day and see if you can fit any short bursts of exercise in. Perhaps you could walk instead of drive, cycle to the train station or take the stairs instead of the lift? Factoring exercise into your existing schedule means you can improve your mental and physical well-being without going too far out of your way.

74

Water flows around obstacles, constantly and effortlessly changing. Studies show that proximity to water improves mood and lowers stress levels, so it's no wonder we love to be near bodies of water. Try visiting a local lake, pond or river and take a moment to appreciate the sounds and the play of light on the water's surface.

75. TRY YOGA

Yoga is an excellent form of calm exercise. The slower you go, the more you get out of it! A regular yoga practice will make you calmer, fitter and more flexible – you could join a local class or browse YouTube for stress-busting sequences. Try these stress-relieving positions to help you wind down – stay in each for 5–12 breaths:

Bàlàsana/Child's pose:
Sit back on your heels and lay your arms by your sides, or stretch them forwards as far as is comfortable.

Janu Sirsasana/
Head-to-knee forward bend:

From a sitting position, extend your right leg out in front of you. Tuck your left foot along your right thigh and bend forward, reaching for your right foot. Swap legs and repeat.

*Kumbhakasana/*Plank pose:

Start on your hands and knees, hands shoulder-width and knees hip-width apart, looking down between your hands. Step back and tuck your toes under, bringing your body into a straight line.

BEING ABLE
TO LET GO, AT
TIMES, IS THE
MOST BEAUTIFUL
OF ALL!

ELIF SHAFAK

76

Talk about what's on your mind with someone you trust. It could be a close friend, a family member or a therapist – pick someone you know is a good listener. They probably won't be able to solve your problems, but often just talking honestly can make things seem more manageable.

77

Binge-watch your favourite feel-good series. The right show will draw you in to its world and immerse you in plots and characters much more complex than those found in films. Throw on your cosiest pyjamas, shut the door on real-world stresses and indulge in an evening of unapologetic vegging-out.

78

Texting, emailing and instant messaging are modern communication miracles, but they can be stressful, ambiguous and impersonal. If you can't see your loved ones in person, a good old-fashioned phone call is the next best thing for fostering connection and understanding. Next time the mood takes you, pick up the phone and have a proper relaxed catch-up with an old friend you don't get to see very often.

79

Dance like no one's watching... and sing along like no one can hear you. Shake your booty in the privacy of your own home or join a dance class and learn a new skill. Moving your body to music releases endorphins and reduces stress. Plus, it's great exercise.

80. UNDERSTAND WHAT YOU CAN AND CANNOT CONTROL

Some things deserve our mental energy – things within our control that need to be thought about and worked out. But there are tons of things we worry about that we have absolutely zero control over. Next time you catch yourself over-thinking, ask yourself whether it's something you can control. If it isn't then it's not worth your time or energy – let it go!

Things you can control:

- Your effort
- Your priorities
- Your responses
- Your actions

Things you can't control:

- Others' opinions
- Others' actions
- The outcome of your effort
- What happens around you

IT ALL DEPENDS ON HOW WE LOOK AT THINGS, AND NOT HOW THEY ARE IN THEMSELVES.

CARL JUNG

81

Speak to yourself like you would a dear friend. Show yourself all the patience, love and understanding you give so readily to others, and don't believe any negative self-talk your inner critic might try on you. If your inner voice is kind, calm and positive you'll be able to find peace within yourself in even the most stressful situation.

82

Go wild swimming – brave the cold of a lake or plunge into the sea. The repetitive nature of swimming has a meditative effect, and the necessity of relaxing your body in order to stay afloat makes it a perfect calm form of exercise.

Research shows that immersing yourself in cold water triggers a flood of mood-boosting neurotransmitters in your brain, forcing your attention out of your head and into your body. Regular cold-water swimming has even been found to increase stress tolerance and to lower levels of the stress hormone cortisol.

83

Forgive yourself. We all make mistakes, and it's easy to dwell on what we would have done differently with hindsight. So give yourself a break! Give yourself permission to be a work in progress and learn from your mistakes. Know that you are always doing your best, and that your best will be different depending on the circumstances.

84

Heart racing? Try blowing on your thumb for four seconds. It sounds silly, but it really works! This weirdly calming life hack works because your thumb has its own pulse. The cooling air slows the pulse and therefore the heart rate. Plus, the act of blowing forces you to deepen your breathing, which has an automatic calming effect on your whole body.

ANXIETY'S
LIKE A ROCKING
CHAIR. IT GIVES YOU
SOMETHING TO DO,
BUT IT DOESN'T GET
YOU VERY FAR.

JODI PICOULT

85. GET YOUR KNITTING NEEDLES OUT

Gentle meditative crafts like knitting or crochet are a wonderful way to create a calm habit wherever you go. Get started with a YouTube tutorial or local knitting group or by asking a crafty friend to teach you. Take pleasure in the rhythmic click-click of the needles and watch as your ball of wool transforms into something useful and beautiful.

Knitting is a perfect way to relax as it allows you to enjoy the process rather than focusing on the end product. Plus, it's incredibly portable – make sure you have your knitting handy and you'll never again be bored on public transport or in the doctor's waiting room.

**EVERY TIME YOU
TAKE A DEEP BREATH
AND MAINTAIN YOUR
TEMPER, YOUR POWER
IS INCREASED.**

NICK OFFERMAN

86

Have a duvet day. The urge to hibernate can be strong, especially in the colder months. Less light makes our bodies produce more melatonin, meaning we need more sleep. While sustained lethargy can be a sign of poor mental or physical health, a duvet day is different. Taking a day to recharge in bed, eat comfort food and generally please yourself can have huge benefits for energy levels and productivity once you return to normal life.

87

A well-known saying goes, "If it's your job to eat a frog, it's best to do it first thing in the morning." Completing your least favourite task first means your day can only improve, so bite the bullet and get that tricky, annoying or unpleasant thing out of the way. Once it's done you can relax and forget about it.

88

Get yourself a stress-squashing mantra. Use whatever works to pull yourself out of a stress-spiral and back into the moment. Once you have your mantra, call upon it when you feel yourself tense up with worry or stress.

Try these and see what feels good:

- Every breath I take fills me with ease
- What will be will be
- This too shall pass

89

Take a hot bubble bath with candles, bath salts, calming music – the whole shebang. The relaxing benefits of bathing are well known, and taking a bath has been shorthand for indulgence and self-care for centuries. Cleopatra knew how to treat herself! It's about much more than getting clean, as regular bathing helps reduce stress and fatigue, as well as improving sleep patterns.

90. BAKE YOURSELF CALM

Many turn to the gentle restorative comforts of baking when they want to relax. Try this super-simple recipe for strawberry yoghurt cake. The best part is that the 150-ml pot of yogurt can be used as a measuring cup for the rest of the ingredients:

150ml natural, full-fat yogurt
    or vegan alternative
2 yogurt pots self-raising flour
1 yogurt pot caster sugar
½ yogurt pot vegetable oil
½ tsp vanilla essence
3 eggs
A handful of strawberries – sliced into slivers
Icing sugar, to serve (optional)

Method:

Pre-heat oven to 180°C/350°F/Gas mark 4, and empty the yogurt into a large bowl.

Wash and dry the yogurt pot, then measure out the flour and sugar and combine it with the yogurt in the bowl.

In a separate bowl beat the oil, vanilla and eggs.

Add the wet ingredients to the dry and stir to combine.

Line a loaf tin with baking parchment and pour in the batter, adding a layer of strawberries halfway through.

Bake for 45 minutes to 1 hour, until a skewer comes out clean.

Leave to cool then top with icing sugar and serve.

You have
to laugh,
especially
at yourself.

MADONNA

91

Turn off all screens and devices an hour before going to bed. The blue light emitted by modern gadgets messes with your sleep cycle and the information overload that comes from a constantly changing internet newsfeed keeps your brain alert when it should be winding down. At least 60 minutes of screen-free time gives you the best chance for a good night's sleep.

92

As you get dressed and undressed, slow down and notice the textures of the fabric and how they feel on your skin. Use calm, unhurried movements. Experiencing sensations mindfully in this way helps you enjoy each moment and keeps your mind from rushing ahead to the next task.

9 3

Find a quiet spot in a park and watch the play of light and shade on the ground. It's easy to give in to the urge to occupy or distract yourself when you're on your own – especially in public. Get comfortable with being idle sometimes – you'll find you notice more of life's small pleasures.

94

Buy yourself flowers. Treat yourself to something beautiful and frivolous simply because you deserve it! Flowers brighten up any room and there's nothing like the scent of freshly cut blooms. Get rid of the idea that you need to wait for someone special to buy you flowers: *you* are someone special.

THE
INSPIRATION
YOU SEEK IS
ALREADY WITHIN
YOU. BE SILENT
AND LISTEN.

RUMI

95. VISUALIZE A CALM ENVIRONMENT

Visualization is a powerful tool for stress reduction because our brains don't distinguish between real experiences and ones we imagine vividly. To visualize, you need to close your eyes and picture a scene that brings you peace and positivity. See it with as much detail as you can. Experience the sounds, smells, sensations and emotions.

In times of stress, try the following visualization:

Imagine yourself in a beautiful meadow. The sun is warm and there's a gentle breeze. No real-world problems or worries exist here. Feel the soft grass beneath you, smell the wildflowers and listen to the birds singing. You can stay in this calm place for as long as you need, and you can visit it any time – it's always there inside you.

96

Look at the sky and notice the colours, textures and quality of light. Humans have long loved to gaze upwards and a sunrise, sunset or full moon is eternally awe-inspiring. Take a moment to appreciate the beauty, mystery and enormity of the universe any time of day or night – there's always something to see.

97

Write a list of all the things you love about yourself – keep it somewhere safe and add to it regularly. Practicing self-love might feel hard or uncomfortable at first, so start with the parts of yourself you find easy to appreciate – perhaps you make a great grilled cheese sandwich, you have lovely shoulders or you're kind to animals. Acknowledge what you like about yourself and watch self-love flourish naturally.

98

Observe the moon every night as it moves through its phases. It's a great reminder that life moves in cycles and we all need to rest and recharge in order to shine. Some believe the moon has a power over people's moods down here on Earth. Why not download a moon calendar app and decide for yourself?

YOU CAN'T CALM THE
STORM, SO STOP TRYING.
WHAT YOU CAN DO
IS CALM YOURSELF.
THE STORM WILL PASS.

TIMBER HAWKEYE

99

Create your own ritual. A ritual can be as simple as a habit – you just have to assign meaning and significance to it. Taking extra care over things you do regularly will help you slow down and appreciate the small, special things in your life. Try adding rituals to your routine such as lighting a particular candle each time you have a bath, or by drinking camomile tea in your favourite mug before bed every evening.

100

If you're struggling to feel calm and it's negatively affecting your life, it might be worth contacting your doctor to talk it through.

There's no shame in asking for help, and there are many solutions available for when stress or anxiety become overwhelming.

Contact a mental-health charity for further advice and support – they have lots of resources and are a good place to start if you want to learn more.

SOMETIMES THE MOST
IMPORTANT THING IN
A WHOLE DAY IS
THE REST WE TAKE
BETWEEN TWO
DEEP BREATHS.

ETTY HILLESUM

If you're interested in finding out more about our books, find us on Facebook at Summersdale Publishers and follow us on Twitter at @Summersdale.

www.summersdale.com

IMAGE CREDITS

Balloon – pp.13, 21, 29, 58, 61, 77, 93, 109, 125, 141, 157 © Mascha Tace/Shutterstock.com
Cloud engraving – pp.32, 43, 56, 72, 96, 112, 155 © grop/Shutterstock.com
Mandala – p.71 © Lovely Mandala/Shutterstock.com
Watercolour wave background and white pinstripe background – pp.14–15, 22–23, 38–39, 46–47, 62–63, 70–71, 86–87, 94–95, 110–111, 118–119, 134–135, 142–143 © Magnia/Shutterstock.com
Yoga figures – pp.118–119 © Babkina Svetlana/Shutterstock.com